AF112251

This Journal Belongs To:

Period(s)

_____

Topic	**Page(s)**
Topic	**Page(s)**

TOPIC	Page(s)

Topic	**Page(s)**

Topic	Page(s)

Topic	Page(s)

N
O
T
E
S

NOTES

NOTES

NOTES

NOTES

NOTES

N
O
T
E
S

NOTES

N
O
T
E
S

NOTES

NOTES

NOTES

NOTES

NOTES

NOTES

NOTES

N
O
T
E
S

NOTES

NOTES

NOTES

NOTES

N
O
T
E
S

NOTES

NOTES

NOTES

NOTES

NOTES

NOTES

www.ingramcontent.com/pod-product-compliance
Lightning Source LLC
LaVergne TN
LVHW061936070526
838199LV00060B/3843